Over in the Jungle

A Rainforest Rhyme

For Emily, Libby, Samantha, Jay, Christina and Will.
Also special thanks to my friend, movement specialist Jean McAdam,
for her ideas on the body movement section of this book. – MB

I dedicate this book to my Grandparents, Navona Pagels and Erwin "Red" & Lenore Martens.
Thank you for your stories and your encouragement and support of my creative endeavors
(and letting me act like a monkey sometimes)! –JC

Artwork created with polymer clay. Original art photographed by Jeff Rose Photography, Inc.

Copyright ©2007 Marianne Berkes
Illustration copyright ©2007 Jeanette Canyon

A Sharing Nature With Children Book

Library of Congress Cataloging-in-Publication Data
Berkes, Marianne Collins.
  Over in the jungle : a rainforest rhyme / by Marianne Berkes ; illustrated by Jeanette Canyon. -- 1st ed.
    p. cm.
  Summary: "A counting and singing approach for young children to learn and appreciate the animals of the
tropical rainforest"--Provided by publisher.
  ISBN 978-1-58469-091-7 (hardback) -- ISBN 978-1-58469-092-4 (pbk.) 1. Rain forest animals--Juvenile
literature. 2. Counting--Juvenile literature. I. Canyon, Jeanette, 1965- ill. II. Title.
  QL112.B45 2007
  591.734--dc22

                                    2006030962

                              Printed in China
                         10 9 8 7 6 5 4 3 2
                              First Edition

                     Design by Jeanette Canyon;
     Computer production by Christopher Canyon and Patty Arnold, Menagerie Design and Publishing.

                           Dawn Publications
                        12402 Bitney Springs Road
                         Nevada City, CA 95959
                            530-274-7775
                         nature@dawnpub.com

Over in the Jungle

A Rainforest Rhyme

By Marianne Berkes

illustrated by Jeanette Canyon

Dawn Publications

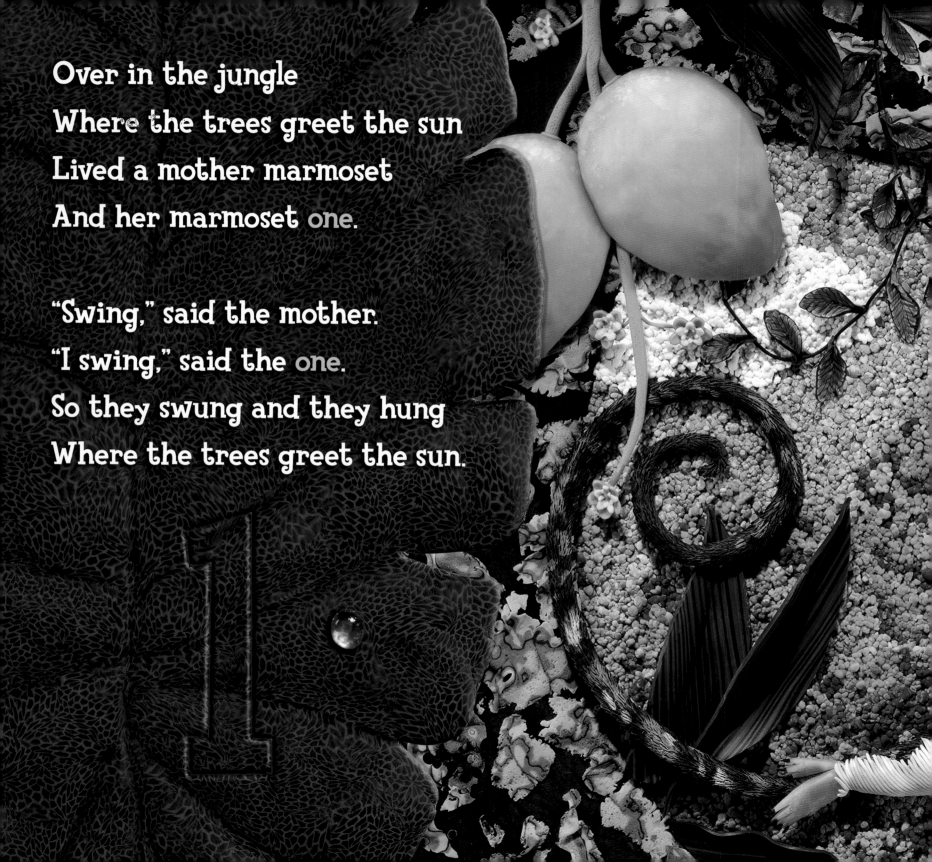

Over in the jungle
Where the trees greet the sun
Lived a mother marmoset
And her marmoset one.

"Swing," said the mother.
"I swing," said the one.
So they swung and they hung
Where the trees greet the sun.

Over in the jungle
Wearing wings of shiny blue
Lived a morpho butterfly
And her little morphos two.

"Flit," said the mother.
"We flit," said the two.
So they flitted and they fluttered
Wearing wings of shiny blue.

Over in the jungle
On a leafy canopy
Lived a noisy mother parrot
And her little parrots three.

"Squawk," said the mother.
"We squawk," said the three.
So they squawked and they walked
On a leafy canopy.

Over in the jungle
On a rainforest floor
Lived a leaf cutter ant
And her little ants four.

"Scurry," said the mother.
"We scurry," said the four.
So they scurried and they hurried
On a rainforest floor.

Over in the jungle
Near a big bee hive
Lived a mother honey bear
And her little honeys five.

"Scramble," said the mother.
"We scramble," said the five.
So they scrambled and they rambled
Toward a big bee hive.

Over in the jungle
Curled around some mossy sticks
Lived a long mother boa
And her little boas six.

"Squeeze," said the mother.
"We squeeze," said the six.
So they squeezed and were pleased
Curled around some mossy sticks.

Over in the jungle
In bromeliad heaven
Lived a poison dart frog
And her little froggies seven.

"Hop," said the mother.
"We hop," said the seven.
So they hopped and they plopped
In bromeliad heaven.

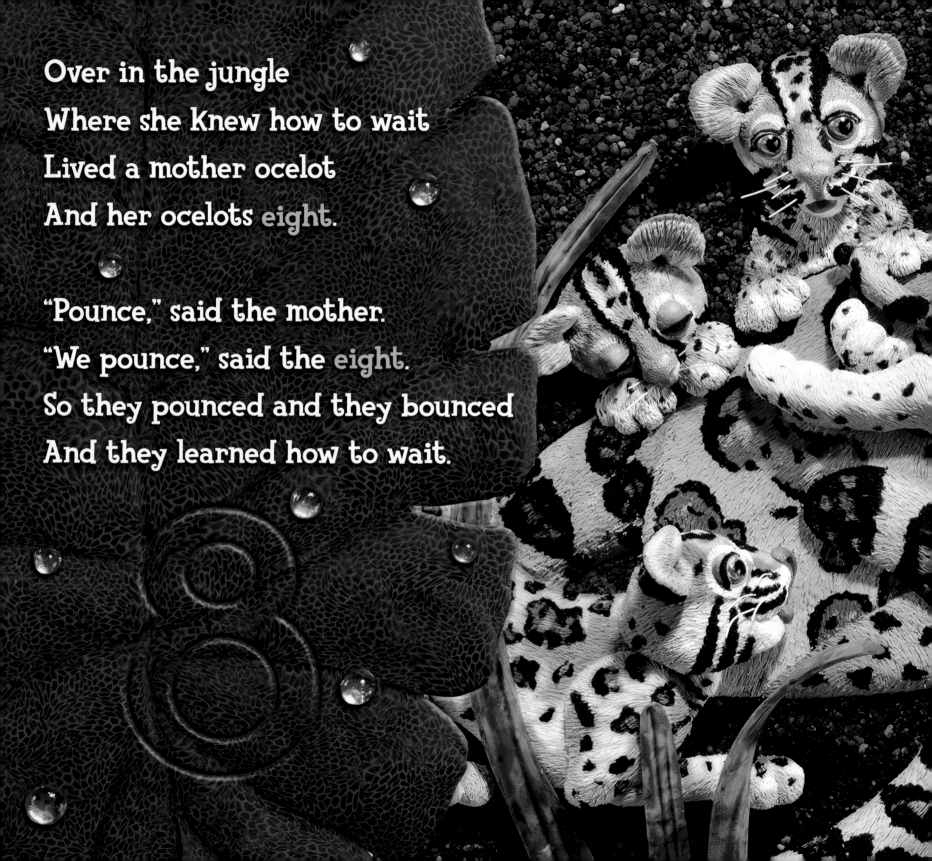

Over in the jungle
Where she knew how to wait
Lived a mother ocelot
And her ocelots eight.

"Pounce," said the mother.
"We pounce," said the eight.
So they pounced and they bounced
And they learned how to wait.

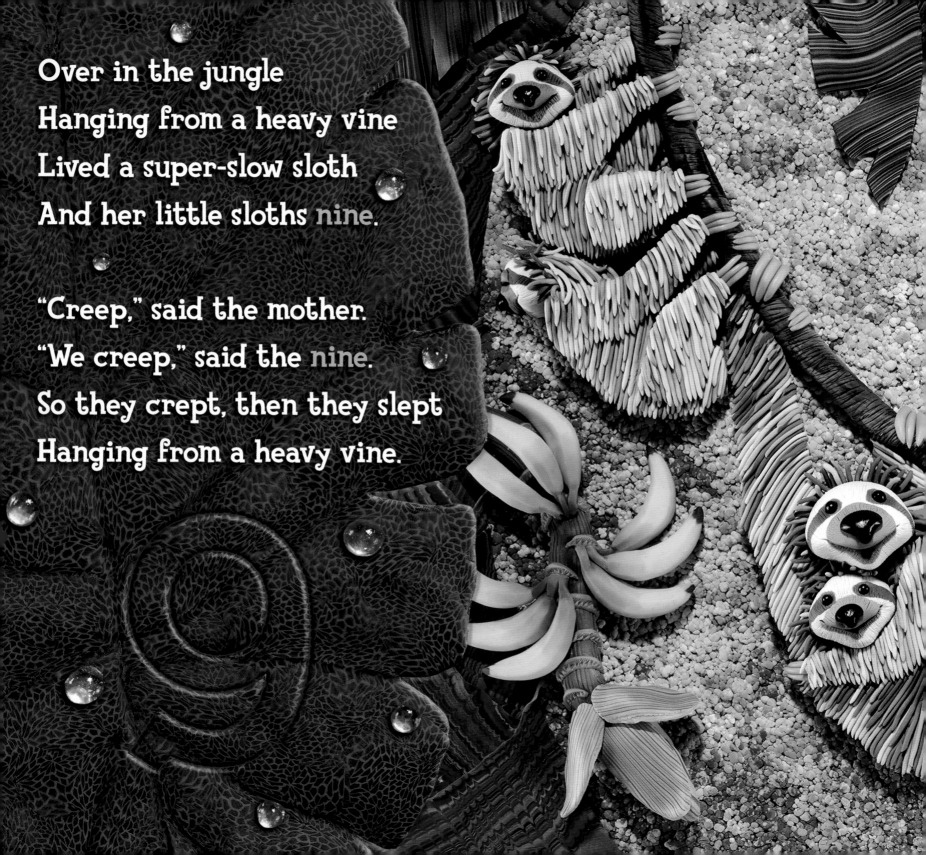

Over in the jungle
Hanging from a heavy vine
Lived a super-slow sloth
And her little sloths nine.

"Creep," said the mother.
"We creep," said the nine.
So they crept, then they slept
Hanging from a heavy vine.

Over in the jungle
In their rainforest den
Lived a father howler monkey
And his little howlers ten.

"Hoot," said the father.
"We hoot," said the ten.
So they hooted and they hollered
In their rainforest den.

10

Over in the jungle, come on, let's take a peek!
In the busy rainforest they're playing hide and seek.
"Find us," say the children.
"From ten to one."
When you find all the creatures then this rhyme is done.

10	Howler Monkeys	5	Honey Bears
9	Sloths	4	Leaf Cutter Ants
8	Ocelots	3	Parrots
7	Poison Dart Frogs	2	Morpho Butterflies
6	Boas	1	Marmoset

Over in the Jungle

Sung to the tune
"Over in the Meadow"

Traditional tune
Words by Marianne Berkes

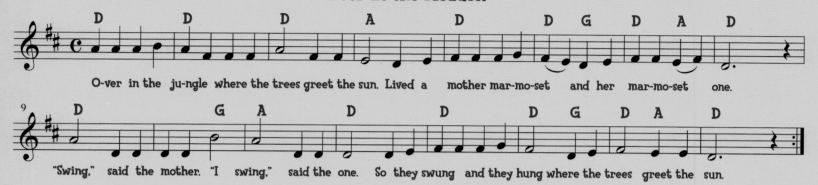

O-ver in the ju-ngle where the trees greet the sun. Lived a mother mar-mo-set and her mar-mo-set one.

"Swing," said the mother. "I swing," said the one. So they swung and they hung where the trees greet the sun.

2. Over in the jungle wearing wings of shiny blue
Lived a morpho butterfly and her little morphos two.
"Flit," said the mother.
"We flit," said the two.
So they flitted and they fluttered wearing wings of shiny blue.

3. Over in the jungle on a leafy canopy
Lived a noisy mother parrot and her little parrots three.
"Squawk," said the mother.
"We squawk," said the three.
So they squawked and they walked on a leafy canopy.

4. Over in the jungle on a rainforest floor
Lived a leaf cutter ant and her little ants four.
"Scurry," said the mother.
"We scurry," said the four.
So they scurried and they hurried on a rainforest floor.

5. Over in the jungle near a big bee hive
Lived a mother honey bear and her little honeys five.
"Scramble," said the mother.
"We scramble," said the five.
So they scrambled and they rambled toward a big bee hive.

6. Over in the jungle curled around some mossy sticks
Lived a long mother boa and her little boas six.
"Squeeze," said the mother.
"We squeeze," said the six.
So they squeezed and were pleased curled around some mossy sticks.

7. Over in the jungle in bromeliad heaven
Lived a poison dart frog and her little froggies seven.
"Hop," said the mother.
"We hop," said the seven.
So they hopped and they plopped in bromeliad heaven.

8. Over in the jungle where she knew how to wait
Lived a mother ocelot and her ocelots eight.
"Pounce," said the mother.
"We pounce," said the eight.
So they pounced and they bounced and they learned how to wait.

9. Over in the jungle hanging from a heavy vine
Lived a super-slow sloth and her little sloths nine.
"Creep," said the mother.
"We creep," said the nine.
So they crept, then they slept hanging from a heavy vine.

10. Over in the jungle in their rainforest den
Lived a father howler monkey and his little howlers ten.
"Hoot," said the father.
"We hoot," said the ten.
So they hooted and they hollered in their rainforest den.

11. Over in the jungle, come on, let's take a peek!
In the busy rainforest they're playing hide and seek.
"Find us," say the children.
"From ten to one."
When you find all the creatures then this rhyme is done.

How Many Babies Do They Really Have?

The story in this book is based upon the popular 19th century song, "Over in the Meadow." In this variation, all the rainforest animals behave as they have been portrayed. That's a fact! But do they have the number of babies as in this rhyme? No, that is fiction.

Animal parents sometimes take care of their babies; sometimes they do not. The mammals in this story nurse their babies, and usually have either one baby (in the case of the honey bear, sloth and howler monkey) or two (marmoset and ocelot). The mother parrot in this story lays two to four eggs and finds food for her babies after they hatch. The mother frog lays eggs which hatch into tiny tadpoles; she then puts the tadpoles into bromeliads for safety, and feeds them until they become frogs. The queen leaf cutter ant lays thousands of eggs in a nest, which she tends until enough worker ants have hatched to take over. Mother boas give birth to live young, to 20 at a time, and the baby snakes fend for themselves immediately. Mother butterflies lay eggs and leave. The eggs develop into caterpillars, which later transform into butterflies. Nature has very different ways of ensuring the survival of different species.

The Rainforest Community

Tropical rainforests are the richest forests on Earth. Even though these lush green forests cover only seven percent of the Earth's land, more than half the world's plants and animals live there. These exotic forests are found in a belt around the equator called the tropics.

There are four layers of tropical rainforest where these animals live. From bottom to top:
    FOREST FLOOR, which is covered with leaf litter, where fungi and insects thrive;
    UNDERSTORY, a darker environment, made up of smaller trees over the ground;
    CANOPY, which is filled with an incredible number of animals because of its thick leafy environment;
    and the
    EMERGENTS, where tops of trees rise above the canopy as high as 200 feet;

Tropical rainforests are so important that they are called the "lungs of the Earth." The trees in the rainforest release oxygen, which we need to breathe. If you want to learn more about this remarkable ecosystem and its creatures, go online to www.rainforest-alliance.org/programs/education. Click on to "kids" and "rainforest resources." And be sure to check out the English/Spanish website of the Children's Eternal Rain Forest in Costa Rica, www.acmcr.org.

About the Rainforest

MARMOSETS are the smallest monkeys in the rainforest, only 7 to 12 inches tall. Their habitat is high trees where they **swing** from tree to tree, grabbing food with their little claws. They eat spiders and other insects as well as fruits, bird's eggs and lizards.

MORPHO BUTTERFLIES are brilliant blue with large wings that catch the light and make them shine. Adult morphos **flit** from one fruit to another, drinking the nectar of rotting fruit with their straw-like proboscis.

PARROTS are noisy, intelligent birds that can always find food in the rainforest because their heavy hooked bills can scoop out fruit and crack seeds. Parrots fly together in pairs or small flocks and like to walk (and **squawk**) in the trees.

LEAF CUTTER ANTS are fascinating rainforest insects. They **scurry** around looking for leaves which they cut and bring back to their underground colonies where they fertilize them with saliva. This causes fungus to grow, which then serves as their food supply.

HONEY BEARS, also called kinkajous, have long tails that they use in climbing as they **scramble** clumsily around the canopy, looking for fruit, insects and honey to eat. Obviously, the furry kinkajou is known as the honey bear because a favorite food, taken from the bees' nests, is honey!

Animals in this Book

BOA CONSTRICTORS are snakes up to 12 feet long. They live in the understory of the rainforest where they eat meat – rats, mice, lizards, fish, birds and wild pigs. When they are ready to strike, their fangs pop out and they **squeeze** their prey.

POISON DART FROG. There are many species of frogs in the rainforest, but the one chosen for this book is the poison dart frog, whose skin is so dangerous that native hunters use it to coat their hunting arrows. The female **hops** long distances to put her tadpole babies into a bromeliad high in the treetops for safety.

OCELOTS are medium-sized spotted cats of Central and South America. They look like small leopards and often stretch out on tree branches, spying on other animals. Graceful, fast hunters, they are most active at night, and **pounce** on their prey.

SLOTHS are slow-moving animals that **creep** around in the canopy. They have long, coarse fur that is so damp that moss and algae grow on it. This helps the sloth hide from its enemies. Sloths spend most of their lives hanging upside-down even when they sleep.

HOWLER MONKEYS are named for their loud, **hooting** calls, which can be heard up to three miles away. The male monkey's roar is the loudest and warns other monkeys to stay away from his territory where his group is living and feeding, mostly on leaves in the canopy.

Tips from the Author

I hope you will read my book often, each time discovering something new and exciting. A great reward, as a visiting children's author and storyteller, is to hear a child shout, "Read it, again!" Over in the Jungle: A Rainforest Rhyme offers many opportunities for extended activities. Here are a few ideas:

- In addition to counting the ten rainforest creatures, what other living things can you find and count?

- Use some of the rainforest animal puppets that are available along with a rain stick as "story stretchers."

- Draw and cut out masks for each rainforest creature. Each child can act out the story with his or her mask.

- Talk about the different layers of the rainforest where the animals live and have the children create a rainforest diorama using polymer or Model Magic clay.

Here is a special treat that I've written for this book. As you sing or read the story, try using different body movements for each animal's action.

Marmosets: Swing right arm across body on the word "swing," then left arm on second "swing". (Arms are now crossed.) Raise them up high on hung and grab the air with fingers.

Morphos: Slowly wave both arms at sides for "flit", then bringing hands together in front, flutter fingers quickly.

Parrots: Stamp right foot on first "squawk"; left foot on second "squawk". Then with tiny sideward steps walk stiffly.

Leaf cutter ants: Get down on hands and feet and quickly scurry to the right and hurry to the left.

Honey bears: With arms at sides, raise one shoulder to ear on "scramble"; then the other.

On "scrambled and rambled", move both shoulders forward in a circular motion.

Boa constrictor: On the floor, curl on one side, stretching arms way out in front and pull in as if squeezing, on the words, "squeezed" and "pleased".

Poison dart frog: Hop on one foot; then the other and quietly fall down on "plop".

Ocelot: Bending forward, place hands under chin as if waiting. Then jump forward on first "pounce" and backward on second "pounce". Then jump up and down on "bounced".

Sloth: Get on back and move shoulders backwards slowly on "creep". On the word "slept", raise legs as if hanging and hold without moving.

Howler monkey: Place one hand under armpit on first "hoot", and other hand under armpit on second "hoot". Now move both arms with hands still under armpits and "hoot and holler."

At the end of the story, children can run and hide on "find us", either to a personal space if they are sitting on a carpet square or to their desks.

Perhaps you can think of other ways to get children actively involved. I would love to hear from teachers and parents with creative ways to use this book. My website is www.MarianneBerkes.com

Tips from the Artist

The illustrations I make for my books are created with polymer clay. As a picture book artist and former early childhood arts educator, I believe that polymer clay is a wonderful, friendly, pliable and colorful media for both children and adults to work with. As a fine artist, I love to create art with an array of colors, patterns and textures, and to make things with my hands—just as children do!

My studio is actually a lot like a kitchen. In a refrigerator I often store my clay. I should say "polymer clay" because it is not like clay dug from the earth, but it is actually a moldable factory-made material that is often referred to as the "new clay". I have a variety of shaping tools including a pasta machine, food processor, cake decorating tools and a variety of recycled objects I fashion into sculpting and texturing tools. And there is even an oven in which the clay is baked after the pictures are pieced together. The original art in this book is not flat, which is very satisfying to me because it speaks to my love of both sculpting and painting. The art is called "relief sculpture": sculptures projecting from a flat surface. To create the two-dimensional illustrations you see in my books, the relief sculptures are photographed (with careful attention to lighting).

Polymer clay offers people of all ages unique ways to communicate and express ideas, as well as to experiment using textures, patterns and colors. You will find many colors available in art and hobby stores - even some translucent and glow-in-the-dark colors. I encourage you to let your imagination soar while you have fun creating your own colorful clay "Jungle Friends"! I would love to see some of your own creations and hear what discoveries you have made. Contact me through the "Authors & Illustrators" section of Dawn Publications' website, www.dawnpub.com.

There are many tools and machines I work with to create my pictures out of polymer clay. One of my favorite gadgets is my food processor. Look at the backgrounds of all of the pictures in this book—I made all of those little balls by tossing different colors of clay into my food processor.

It's fun to work with molds. Sometimes I create molds out of polymer clay and sometimes I mold my clay around objects to capture their shapes, patterns and textures. For the butterflies in this book I created their wings by molding very thin layers of clay over seashells.

I love sculpting with polymer clay. I use my fingers and lots of different sculpting tools to shape and form the subjects in my pictures. Here I am using small knitting needles to sculpt the face of one of the howler monkeys. Some of my sculpting tools are very tiny so I can create fine little details in places where my fingers are too big.

Research is often an important part of creating my art. I go to libraries, museums—and anyplace I can go to learn about the subject matter in my pictures. I also do a lot of research using my computer but my favorite way to do research is going out in nature. Much of my research for this book was done by visiting a zoo and conservatory close to my home.

Marianne Berkes has spent much of her life with young children as a teacher, children's theater director and children's librarian. She knows how much children enjoy brilliantly illustrated counting books with predictable text about real animals. Recently retired to write full time and visit schools and libraries, she is also the author of the award-winning *Over in the Ocean: In a Coral Reef.*

Jeanette Canyon creates her colorful and beautifully textured relief sculptures with polymer clay. Unbounded imagination and a belief in unlimited creative possibilities are the motivations that shape her innovative approach to the award winning children's books she designs and illustrates. Her great talent as a fine artist, coupled with her experience as a former arts educator of young children are the foundational attributes that have influenced her critically acclaimed art and picture books. Jeanette Canyon received her BFA from the Columbus College of Art & Design in Columbus, Ohio where she resides with her husband Christopher Canyon—also a creator of many children's books. When she isn't working in her studio she spends her time visiting schools and libraries, speaking at conferences and sharing her joyful and creative spirit with others.

ALSO BY MARIANNE BERKES AND JEANETTE CANYON

Over in the Ocean: In a Coral Reef — With their unique and outstanding style, Marianne and Jeanette portray the vivid community of creatures that inhabit the ocean's coral reefs. Its many awards include Teaching Magazine's Teacher's Choice Award for Best Children's Book; the Gold Award from NAPPA (National Assoc. for Parenting Publications); the Bank Street College of Education Best Children's Book of the Year; and the Marion Vannett Ridgway Memorial 2005 Honor Book Award.

A SAMPLING OF NATURE AWARENESS BOOKS FROM DAWN PUBLICATIONS

City Beats: A Hip Hoppy Pigeon Poem by S. Kelly Rammell, illustrated by Jeanette Canyon. See and feel a pulsing city from the unique perspective of a pigeon! Dramatically illustrated with clay art.

The John Denver & Kids Series — John Denver's most child-friendly and nature-aware lyrics are adapted and illustrated as picture books by Christopher Canyon. Currently in release: *Sunshine On My Shoulders, Take Me Home, Country Roads, Grandma's Feather Bed,* and *Ancient Rhymes: A Dolphin Lullaby.*

Eliza and the Dragonfly by Susie Caldwell Rinehart, illustrated by Anisa Claire Hovemann, a charming story of a girl and a dragonfly, each experiencing their own metamorphosis. Winner of the 2005 International Reading Assn. award for Best Picture Book.

Seashells by the Seashore by Marianne Berkes, illustrated by Robert Noreika. Children comb the beach, counting and identifying shells, and appreciating the creatures that lived in them.

Dawn Publications is dedicated to inspiring in children a deeper understanding and appreciation for all life on Earth. To view our titles or to order, please visit us at www.dawnpub.com, or call 800-545-7475.